A Little of Wha

'ETER DOYLE'S ANSWER TO CHOLESTEROL

Peter Doyle with Taffy Davies

Cartoons by Max Foley

SALLY MILNER PUBLISHING

First published in 1990 by
Sally Milner Publishing Pty Ltd
17 Wharf Road
Birchgrove NSW 2041 Australia

© Taffy Davies & Peter Doyle 1990

Production by Sylvana Scannapiego
Cover by David Constable
Illustrations by Max Foley
Typeset in 13/15 pt Paladium by
Trade Graphics Pty Ltd, Melbourne
Printed in Australia by
Australian Print Group
Printed on **RE&RIGHT** 100% Re-cycled Paper

National Library of Australia
Cataloguing-in-Publication data:

Doyle, Peter.
    A little of what you fancy.

    Includes index
    ISBN 1 86351 004 4.

    1. Low-cholesterol diet. 2. Low-cholesterol diet-
    Recipes. I. Davies, Taffy. II. Foley, Max, 1944–
    III. Title.

613.28

Distributed in Australia and New Zealand exclusively by
Transworld Publishers

Healthy Diet Pyramid reproduced with permission from
Australian Nutrition Foundation Inc
Copyright 1989 Australian Nutrition Foundation Inc

Front cover photograph: Tim Bauer/Australian Magazine

'This is an easy to read, inspiring book. It shows that the healthy way is not difficult. Delicious food, exercise, family and friends can all be enjoyed together — with the bonus of a healthier heart.'

Dr Hodges
Director
National Heart Foundation

I must thank Beverley Davies for all her hard work on the recipes in this book.

Contents

Contents

Half a Dozen Blokes in a Boat

This book began as the result of a fishing trip. There were half a dozen of us in the boat, middle-aged blokes — give or take a decade or two — all keen to catch a decent feed of fish. It was when we were about an hour away from the fishing ground that it began to dawn on me that no-one was talking fishing.

Now, when you're only an hour or so from the spot, the conversation just has to be about who's going to boat the first decent snapper (and the odd bet or two about who buys the drinks as a result). Will Bob catch more than the little coral trout he managed last time out? What bait are we going to use? Which way is the wind coming and what marks are we going to line up on?

There'll be a cup of tea coming up (a bit early to crack open a grog yet) and people will be looking to rods and reels and lines. Not today, however.

No, there was quite a different discussion

1

going on. George, a funny joker from Western Australia, and not a bad fisherman, George said he'd just had his cholesterol reading and the results he'd received had prompted him to start thinking about going on a diet. His reading was up over the six mark.

'Six?' said Theo. 'My reading's up over seven. My doctor reckons I have to lose two stone, get off the butter, give up alcohol, no prawns, no meat. I tell you, a man might as well be dead, if you ask me.'

Then it was Bob's turn to weigh in. He's got to be the fittest of the lot of us. He's been off the grog a couple of years now and on the Pritikin diet; he's as active as a fiddler's elbow, plays sport — some sports better than others admittedly, but he still has a go — and he works like a bastard. Not everyone likes what he does (it's not every prime minister who can please all the people all of the time, as someone once said), but he does work. 'I've got a cholesterol problem myself,' he said. 'Got to watch what I eat, and that's not easy when you're out at all these official functions.'

Bob wasn't giving his cholesterol count away, but I thought I'd top the rest of them easily. 'What are you blokes on about? I've just had my reading and it's come out at nine.'

That seemed to really impress them. 'Nine?' said Michael. 'Nine? You should be dead, you bugger.'

He was only half joking — and he's not a doctor. But all this started me thinking. Here we were, a group of men and all suffering with a cholesterol problem. All of us were unhappy about it. Bob seemed to be working on his through the Pritikin diet, but no-one else had made much of an effort to really do anything about it.

The conversation kicked on. We were all aware of the problem; we were all aware that we *should* do something about it, but by and large the regimens our doctors had drawn up for us were too demanding or hard to follow or called for major sacrifices of things that we considered to be very much a part of 'the good life'. And as the last member of the party, Michael, said, 'If you have to give up the good life, you might as well be dead.' He had tried to battle through a couple of books telling him what cholesterol is and what to do about it, but he found that he got bogged down in charts and calorie counts and scientific stuff, which he supposed was all well and good, but he really couldn't cope with it, so he gave up.

'All I want to do,' he said (and it sounded pretty reasonable to me), 'is to be sensible about it, get the cholesterol down and *still* enjoy life to the fullest extent. That's not too much to ask, is it?'

Poor old Michael! And, we all agreed with

him. What was the point of prolonging an existence we weren't going to enjoy?

As we reached the fishing spot and I lined the boat up — 'Let go the anchor when I give you the word, Bob' — I began to think of writing a book for these blokes, people like my friends, people like you.

I've learnt a bit about cholesterol and weight loss over the past few years, but what you are going to get is not a medical treatise, though we have asked a couple of doctors to run an eye over the manuscript to make sure we don't actually kill anyone. What you're getting is a book telling you what I have learned about cholesterol, how I've been able to cope with it without too much effort or discomfort and how I am here still enjoying the good things in life like cheese and prawns and meat, and . . . well, all the good things they say you should not even look at.

Oh, by the way, while I'm having a ball and looking forward to a lusty few years before I go to the Great Fishing Ground In the Sky, I have just had my latest cholesterol count. It's down to five. My doctor's happy with me, and I'm pretty pleased with myself, too. So come on and share my pleasure.

And if you really can't wait until you get to the end of the book to find out what a millimole is, turn to page 80.

Be Positive

Do you remember those embroidered mottoes Grannie used to hang on the living room wall? 'Bless This House' and 'God is the unseen guest at the table' and more of the like. Remember?

I've been thinking of getting one made for myself. It would read:

'If die I must, then die I shall — but first I'm going to live.'

My old dad has a saying, too. He reckons it doesn't matter what sort of a day it is ... as long as you're here to enjoy it, there's a lot who would swap it with you.

Now what has all this got to do with cholesterol and losing weight, and all those grave reasons that made you buy this book in the first place?

Plenty.

Because, as I've already mentioned, this book is about how one person — yours truly, your old mate Pete — is living with a cholesterol problem, with a triglyceride problem and with a weight problem, and is still enjoying life.

Wouldn't be dead for quids, as they say.

The secret is, you've got to be positive. I mean, practically any day of the week you can pick up a paper or watch a television news bulletin and discover that there's something else we're not supposed to eat — there's mercury in the fish and pesticides in your steak, oranges are up to their navels in toxic sprays, nuts and fruits are going to get you if the milkshakes don't, and so on, and so on. Strewth, if you stopped eating all the things they reckon are no good for you, you'd end up eating bloody nothing. You might as well pack it in on the spot.

For inspiration, I can, of course, take a look at my mum and dad and see as sprightly a pair of senior citizens as you'll come across on a long day's hike — and both come from families with a history of heart problems and high cholesterol. As I've discovered, you can learn to live with these things and still live the good life.

Take Mum. (Dad's no slouch, but it's Mum who's the real goer.) Mum's into her eightieth year and, despite the fact that she has suffered with high cholesterol all her life, she's a walking monument. She's still the matriarch; she still finds time to write a book; and she still cooks and eats a lovely baked dinner.

So my message is that it's still possible to live an enjoyable life to the full, despite your high

6

cholesterol. You don't have to give up all the good things and become mealy mouthed into the bargain. But what you need, first and foremost, is to believe that it's possible.

And that's what I mean by being positive.

Know Thine Enemy

Do you remember the story about Field Marshal Montgomery during the second world war? When he was fighting Rommel in the desert, he was supposed to have hung a portrait of the German commander in his caravan so he could study it at least once a day. A real case of 'Know thine enemy'.

I'm not actually going to show you a portrait of our enemy, cholesterol, though I could if I liked. My mum's got a bottle full of the stuff at home just to serve as a grisly reminder of the evil little stuff that almost gave her a cerebral haemorrhage. It is not a pretty sight. Now I'm not trying to scare the wits out of you here, just trying to give you an idea of what our enemy can actually do.

So what is this stuff we are all so worried about, this cholesterol? It's funny stuff, cholesterol. Funny peculiar, that is. Or at least it would be, if it wasn't that it can kill you.

And here's the paradox. Your body actually produces cholesterol of its own accord; it is part of the structure that helps build cells and helps keep your body together. Now that, obviously, isn't going to kill anyone. So the first thing to realise is that some cholesterol is actually good for you, vital in fact. If we didn't have some cholesterol in our bodies we'd actually be in pretty bad shape.

The problem really begins when the levels of the cholesterol in your body rise above the amount that is actually good for you. Under normal circumstances your liver will get rid of tiny surpluses but if the surplus builds up it can't cope; the surplus has to go somewhere, and since it is travelling around in the bloodstream that is exactly where it stays. One bit sticks to an artery wall, a bit more sticks to that and before you know where you are you've got a build up. Your blood can't flow properly and you've got troubles.

It's a bit like a river when a tree branch gets stuck. Another gets stuck on the first, then all sorts of gunk starts building up behind it and it's not too long before the river is dammed and water below the blockage is down to a trickle. The only solution is to get rid of the blockage, probably with a stick of dynamite or the help of a bulldozer.

Same with cholesterol. You've got to get rid of it, unclog the artery streams so that your blood can do what your blood's got to do. The snag is that you can't take a stick of dynamite or a

Attempting to unclog the artery streams

bulldozer to the cholesterol in your arteries. You've got to break it down bit by bit.

There's the essence of it in a nutshell. So how do we set about unclogging our arteries? Well, the first step is to find out how we manage to get all that cholesterol into our body to begin with.

HOW THE ENEMY GETS THERE

Let's be realistic. How do we get most things into our body in the first place? Right, hands up all those who said, 'Through what we eat.' Well done, you two. Does that sound too obvious? Do you think your old mate Pete's being a right bloody smartie? Because I'm not really. The point is that a lot of people think cholesterol build-up — bad cholesterol, that is — just happens. It doesn't. It happens as a result of what we eat.

And here's another surprise: those foods that have a lot of cholesterol in them are not necessarily the big villains. I'm talking here about things like lobster and prawns, a decent steak, eggs...you know, the usual gang of suspects. What normally happens is that although your body absorbs a little of the cholesterol you take in with your food, it will eliminate most of the surplus.

The trouble is more likely to come when you

11

eat foods high in fats. Your body turns that fat into cholesterol — and that's the rotten stuff that gets into your bloodstream and can start building up. So it's the fat you eat that is more of a problem than the foods that are high cholesterol, not that I'm saying they can't be a problem, too.

Let's look at that again, because this is important. If you eat foods which have cholesterol in them, sure your cholesterol will rise because your body will absorb some of that cholesterol. But it will not rise as high as if you eat fatty foods, because your body will turn the fat into cholesterol and that's when we really need to do something about the stuff.

Be careful, though. I am not telling you to go out and start living the life of Riley, hoeing into crabs and cutlets and cheese and all that stuff. You do that and you might well end up dying the death of Riley, and we don't want that, do we?

What I am saying is that you can still eat these things, you can still enjoy the good things, but one of my key words, a word that you'll find cropping up again and again throughout this book, is moderation. We'll come to all of that later in the piece; in the meantime, take it easy.

WHAT HAVE WE LEARNT SO FAR?

• Cholesterol is a waxy-fatty substance and too much of it can clog up the arteries.

• A certain amount of cholesterol is good; our body needs it to function properly. What we don't need is an excess of cholesterol that our body can't get rid of.

• Not all foods containing cholesterol are necessarily bad for us, and while we can eat them, we cannot pig out on them if we want to get something back from the government in the way of an old age pension.

• The real nasty is fat.

And here, as they say, endeth the first lesson.

Pete Confesses All

I suppose I had better declare an interest before this book goes much further. I am in the seafood business; I keep body and soul together by selling seafood at Sydney Fish Markets and fish and chips (and one or two other dishes) at a couple of restaurants.

I can see you all asking what's a bloke like me doing writing about cholesterol when I'm out there flogging prawns and oysters and crabs and all those other good things. Good question. The answer, of course, is that all these good things aren't going to wipe you out — IF you follow my advice and eat all things in moderation. Let's face it, there aren't many people around who can afford to eat lobster on a daily basis and anyone looking at cholesterol levels would be pretty damn stupid to try, even if they could afford it.

As I've said before, moderation is the go. Sure you can eat all the good things, but don't overdo any of them, and lay off for a while (like a good long while) after you've had a feed. Sure I said that your body will eliminate surplus cholesterol, but it's not going to cope too well with a big overload.

It's the same thing with meat. We'll talk about meat a bit later, but the theme is unchanging: if you eat steak and eggs for breakfast, two lamb chops for lunch and then roast beef, three vegies and gravy for dinner, you are going to overdose on fat and protein for sure.

I know that used to be a traditional Aussie meal structure, but while it may bring back memories of Australia's proud bush past, it isn't doing anything for our health today.

But let's get back to the fish. Yes, I am in the seafood caper and yes, I know that some seafoods are not as brilliant for you as others. I also know that some fish are very good for you indeed. And much as I'd like to suggest that everyone go out and buy only the most expensive fish around, I must report that some of the best fish for you are from the distinctly cheaper end of the range. Don't believe me? Try trevally, mullet and redfish, three oily fish, for starters.

Now here's a story and a half for you. Next time you go out for dinner don't bore your friends with the latest news about your cholesterol count — no matter how good it is — tell them about the Eskimos and how they rarely die of sudden heart failure. Do you know why? It's because they eat oily fish. Lots of it. The oil in the fish keeps

Eskimos stay fit on oily fish

their blood thin. Indeed, it has been alleged that in the days when the Vikings went about attacking various nations their Eskimo victims used to bleed to death from surface wounds because their blood would not clot quickly enough to prevent it.

Then consider the Japanese. They're reckoned to have the least amount of heart disease of any race, and consider the amount of seafood they eat. Coincidence or cause and effect? Or could it be that they are fairly small eaters, early exponents of the Doyle theory — eat what you like, in moderation? Whatever the answer, I'm telling you this about the Japanese and the Eskimos because while it may not have a great deal to do with cholesterol it does have a bearing on the same thing — helping to save you from keeling over with a heart attack.

The oil that keeps the Eskimos chipper through the long Arctic nights is exactly the same sort of oil found in those three little beauties — tuna, mullet and garfish.

So what is it about Eskimos and fish fat? Danish researchers got onto the story back in the 1970s. They could not understand why the Eskimos weren't wiped out by heart attacks — they were doing all the wrong things from a dietary point of view, or so it seemed. They were getting 40 per cent of their calories from fat and it was animal fat into the bargain — fish, seal, walrus and whale. Not only that, they weren't eating anywhere near what is considered a reasonable amount of fresh fruit and vegies (well, living in Greenland you can understand that).

Yet their hearts were doing well. Heredity? It didn't seem so. But then researchers established an interesting point — Eskimos moving from Greenland to Denmark and taking up the eating habits of the Danes soon had heart attack rates similar to those of the Danes.

It soon became clear that the difference lay in the type of fat the Eskimos were eating in Greenland — their so-called polyunsaturated fatty acids have a different structure from those usually found in Western diets. The fats found in the typical Western diet are known as the Omega-6 variety. The Eskimos have Omega-3.

Without getting too technical, what happens to people eating a typical Western diet is this: the body uses polyunsaturated fatty acids to produce an agent called a prostaglandin. It reacts on small cells in the blood which are involved in preventing clotting, making the cells sticky so they form blood clots more easily.

At the same time a balance is struck by the artery wall using the same fatty acids to produce another prostaglandin which counteracts the clotting process. The action and reaction are a bit more complex than that, of course, but that's the essence of it. It's when that balance is disturbed that things start to get decidedly tricky.

Now, enter Omega-3. When the diet is high in these fatty acids, the small cells produce a different type of prostaglandin, one which does not cause the small cells to stick and form clots.

In May 1987 *Australian Family Physician* published an article with a heading saying fish oil fatty acids were the answer to heart disease. I'm not going to tackle an outfit as heavy as *Australian Family Physician* but I would say that perhaps not all the evidence is in yet. Omega-3 may well be a move in the right direction, but I don't really see it as a miracle cure-all. Yet.

So there it is. A fascinating story — well, I think it is a fascinating story — and one we can undoubtedly learn from. And my finny friends, trevally, redfish and mullet? They're high in Omega-3, that special 'secret ingredient' of the Eskimos.

You'll find a recipe or two for these fish in the section at the back, but I can tell you now that I am very fond of my fried fish and you can fry these three very easily, and eat them with no problems. A mullet fillet is dead simple — toss a couple in a little flour just to give them a coating, and place in a frying pan with a little grapeseed or olive oil. Cook for five minutes and you've got a top feed. By the way, avoid mullet caught in muddy rivers during late winter and early summer; they have an earthy taste.

The humble mullet — would you believe it?

And an intriguing thing about Australian fish has been reported in a pamphlet put out by the New South Wales Fish Marketing Authority called 'New South Wales Seafood is Heart Food'. Omega-3 is found in fish throughout the world, but Australian fish are unique in that they contain both Omega-3 and Omega-6. The Authority offers a cautious line: 'As both these fatty acids are thought to help protect against heart disease, there is value in eating fresh seafood from all New South Wales waters,' (and presumably other Australian waters as well).

The pamphlet is full of lots of other splendid advice, too.

Like various other food authorities, however, the fish people also have to acknowledge that some of their products have not had a very good press in recent years. Let's quote them on squid and prawns, which 'have the highest cholesterol and this has given them a bad reputation in the past. However, they are still low in fat and there is no reason to omit them from the diet. **Large quantities may need to be avoided.**' The emphasis is mine, but the message is still the same — eat in moderation. If you go to town on something, lay off it for some time. And do note that some of the seafoods singled out — e.g. squid, prawns and ocean perch — are high in cholesterol (in every 100 grams of squid there are 160 milligrams and 0.9 grams of fat; for king prawns it's 170 milligrams of cholesterol and 1.0 gram of fat, and ocean perch has 120 milligrams of cholesterol and 1.5 grams of fat), but we are talking about cholesterol here, not fat. That's the important difference.

Of all the fish listed orange roughy is given the highest fat rating — 7.2 grams per 100 grams — and gemfish has 6.4 grams per 100, but most fish in the Authority charts have under two grams per 100 grams.

SUMMARY

• The structure of fatty acids can vary. The typical Western diet contains fats of the variety called Omega-6.
• The Eskimos for years have eaten oily fish, which has Omega-3 fatty acids, yet despite their high animal fat diet, they rarely die of heart failure. Omega-3 fats produce a prostaglandin which does not cause the blood to clot, and this reduces the likelihood of heart problems.
• Trevally, redfish and mullet are all high in Omega-3, in fact all Australian fish are unique

in that they contain both Omega-3 and Omega-6. Australian fish is therefore a good product to assist the war against heart disease.

• Although some seafood such as squids, prawns and ocean perch are high in cholesterol, they are low in fat and so can still be eaten in moderation.

Did Somebody Mention the Word 'Weight'?

Unfortunately a cholesterol problem often seems to go hand in hand with a weight problem, so not only do we have to try to lower the cholesterol we've also got to do something about the weight. On the more fortunate side, often tackling one problem seems to help take care of the other one. But that's where the hard bit comes in, you say — tackling either problem. Well I'll tell you a little about my experiences.

When the doc first started talking to me about losing weight I wasn't all that inclined to believe him. I mean, I was doing nicely, living life to the full, enjoying everything that was going. I reckon Moses could have come up with a couple more commandments based on my indulgences alone. But then I stopped to think. The doc wasn't doing himself any favours telling me to get my weight down, to keep an eye on the cholesterol level. So, yes, I had to concede, he knew what he was doing and what he was saying was for my benefit and not his. I reckoned it this way: if a bloke can't take notice of warnings issued by a bloke's own doc and a bloke's own body, then a bloke's a bloody mug.

I decided to give it all a go. First thing I did was to make sure that I really did want to do it, because I realised if I was half-hearted about it I'd probably already lost the battle. Did I want to do it? Yes. Definitely? Absolutely, positively. Why? Because I was — am — enjoying this life too much to turn up my toes at this stage of the game.

The next thing I thought I'd better do was figure out how much weight I was going to be able to lose. I reckoned that if I could get my weight down by about thirty kilos I could keep it like that, and feel a lot better for it. But I knew I'd be living in a bit of a fantasy world if I thought I could do that overnight. No, that was aiming for the stars, and the earth was still looking pretty appealing to me. An achievable goal, that was what I had to give myself. And this is a very important point: if you set yourself an achievable goal, you won't get despondent about not having been able to reach your target.

I settled on ½ kilo a week. Nothing spectacular, but something attainable and enough to be noticed, if only on the bathroom scales. But, as I'm sure you'll agree, I had a lot to lose. If you

Take a good hard look at yourself

have less to lose, it is sometimes slower coming off, so set your sights a bit lower.

So, how do we go about losing weight?

Once you've decided how much you'd like to lose, you've got to psyche yourself up. You've got to own up to the fact that you are overweight.

Go and get a photograph of yourself, a sideways shot, with your big flabby gut hanging out — no, don't pretend that you've just got a slight pot as the result of a rather large lunch — come on, be honest. Right, take a good hard look at yourself. Do you agree now that you are overweight? Good.

Okay, stick that photo in the bathroom where you can see it every day. Not your actual Bo Derek or Mike Douglas, are you? But hang in there. We can't transform a goose into a swan, but we can improve matters.

Second, if you don't already have a set, go out and buy yourself a cheap pair of bathroom scales. We want to measure our daily progress. (I know, lots of people tell you not to weigh yourself daily, but I find that jumping on the scales every day keeps your mind on the job. There's no chance of saying you'll improve by weigh in time next Wednesday . . .) I'd go for a pair of electronic scales myself. You can't cheat and wind back the dials on those. But no leaning casually against the wall, or standing on them with only one foot.

Next, visit your doctor or dietitian and get him or her to run up an eating plan for you. If you don't want to do that, you can go for a well-known diet, if you like. Perhaps something like the Pritikin diet, although I must say I'd give that one a miss myself. I mean, my God, some people on the Pritikin look bloody horrible — positively gaunt. Not all of them, of course — Bob Hawke's on the Pritikin and he's looking good. But, even so, it's not for me. You have to change your lifestyle too dramatically for my liking, and that's just what I didn't want to do. I wanted to go on eating out, going out and enjoying myself.

Another thing you could try is Weight Watchers. Their diet can be adapted to almost any lifestyle. But it's a good idea to check with your doctor first. However, if you think you feel a little akin to my philosophies on life I'd suggest you follow my sensible eating plan, which I outline a bit later.

When I finally admitted to myself that I had better do something about losing weight, I started to think seriously about what I ate. I realised that I wasn't prepared to give up some of my greatest pleasures — like my weekly roast leg of lamb. And I worked out a way that I didn't have to. I don't need to keep it a deep, dark secret;

A little of what you fancy

I'm happy to share it with you. Actually, I think we may be setting a world record here (are you listening, Mr Guinness?); I don't know of another cholesterol book in which the first recipe is for a good old traditional Aussie roast lamb. But when you love something enough, a way can be found — even for someone like me with a cholesterol problem. I wasn't going to let that stop me from having one of my favourite meals.

Roast lamb

1 leg lamb (about 2 kg), trim off fat
1 clove garlic, cut in slivers
1 tablespoon fresh or dried rosemary leaves
1 pepper, freshly ground
1 cup water

Wipe lamb with paper towel. Make small slits in skin and insert garlic slivers. Rub with the rosemary and pepper. Pour water into baking dish and place lamb thick side up on a rack in the dish. Cook in a hot oven (200° C) for 10 to 15 minutes, to brown meat. Reduce heat to 180° C and cook for a further 1¾ hours, turning once. Baste occasionally with pan juices.

When the meat is cooked, wrap it in foil and rest the leg for about 15 minutes in a warm place.

While the lamb is resting, stick the pan juices in the freezer for 10 minutes. This will cause the fat to thicken on top of the juices. Chuck the fat away — go on, chuck it away (and don't you feel better already?) — then use the rest of the pan juices to make your gravy.

Serve with steamed vegetables and don't forget the mint sauce.

Being able to enjoy a meal like this is, of course, the entire point of this book: you can still lose weight; you can still keep your cholesterol count down; you can lower your triglycerides; and you can do all that while still eating just about anything you like. Bloody hell, I've seen some people with a cholesterol problem who have become so afraid of food they just about exist on a dry biscuit and a glass of distilled water. They look at a prawn as if it is going to bite them, they toy with a beautiful steak and refuse to have anything to do with cheese.

Well, based on my experiences I'd say that was a lot of taurean fertiliser. Unless, repeat unless, you are already at death's door with cholesterol and you have the entire College of Surgeons telling you not to eat something, I'd reckon you can just about eat anything. But in moderation.

Moderation. That's the message I'll keep on hammering here. Moderation — a little of what you fancy.

MODERATION

Moderation in all foods

PETE'S SENSIBLE EATING PLAN

There was nothing planned or rigorous about my food schedule. For the most part I was able to eat what I liked. Breakfast usually consisted of a bowl of Uncle Toby's oats with low-fat milk, a banana and tea. There was no sugar. I gave up sugar 10 years ago and I've lost the craving for it now. Then throughout the morning there would be more tea. Sometimes I'd have it with some low-fat milk and other times I'd have it black.

Lunch for me was a dawdle (my change in eating habits provided a good excuse to get out of many of those business bashes). I like tuna tinned in oil, love the stuff. While I was knocking the weight off I'd have a tin of tuna for lunch five days out of seven. I'd drain the oil off and make two rounds of sandwiches with wholemeal bread (no butter) and throw in a tomato or onion for variety. I'd also have another cup of tea and half an hour later I'd have a bit of fruit.

On other days I'd have a different line in sandwiches — asparagus, cold meat, salad. But always the four slices of wholemeal bread, cup of tea and a piece of fruit later.

For dinner I'd have my roast lamb one night of the week, of course making sure that I always roasted it on a rack in a baking dish so that the fat fell through and was discarded before the gravy was made. Another dinner would consist of cold leftover roast and salad. For the rest of the week I'd go for things like a steak with no fat or a piece of fish — jewfish, tuna steaks, whiting, tailor — grilled or pan fried in a little grapeseed oil, depending on my fancy or what was available. Plus vegies, of course.

Maybe I am a man of simple pleasures, but that food plan — if that's not too grandiose a name for it — helped me lose weight, lots of it. It wasn't the greatest thrill of my gastronomic career, but I survived those few months and now I am finding it no problem at all to maintain that weight. I may still have the odd splurge at night — a Chinese blowout somewhere (recently I had Peking duck and loved every tasty mouthful) or roast beef and Yorkshire pud at a friend's place. Come winter I'm looking forward to a big, thick, hearty stew made from mutton neck chops. That's even tastier than a roast leg of lamb.

Of course my particular culinary tastes are not those of everyone, so I'll just let you know the general guidelines I followed and you can modify the plan to suit your own tastes. One important thing you must remember is to eat three proper meals a day. That way you won't get hungry and be tempted to eat too much of those things you should only eat in moderation. It's those little

snacks that can be your downfall.

Believe it or not, pyramid power can have a lot to do with good nutrition. The sort of pyramid I'm talking about has nothing to do with the mystical powers of the ancient Egyptians and their Pharaohs. The pyramid I'm talking about is the Healthy Diet Pyramid, an idea dreamed up by the Australian Nutrition Foundation. And my thanks to the Foundation people for letting us use it here.

The concept is simple. It lays out in graphic form the proportions of basic foods you should eat to maintain a healthy lifestyle. The things you can eat most of, at the bottom of the pyramid, include vegetables, bread, cereals and, if you like that sort of thing, dried peas, beans and lentils. Not really my cup of tea, though, I'm afraid. And, in case you didn't realise, pasta is included in this lot, too. But don't go smothering it with rich, creamy sauces. There are plenty of vegetables and herbs that you can use to make a delicious pasta sauce, not to mention the occasional seafood variety — just remember that word moderation. Fruit is also included in this section.

The next group up has lean meat, poultry (with the skin off — and no cheating), eggs, fish, nuts, and low-fat dairy products — milk, yoghurt and cheese, but not too much of these — and don't eat a little bit of each one all at once, that's not quite the idea. As I've already mentioned, some studies now indicate that fish may have heart health benefits so I'm pleased to say that I obviously had it right all along with my tuna sandwiches for lunch and fish for dinner several nights a week.

Towards the top of the pyramid are things like butter, margarine and oil. The pyramid doesn't say, 'Don't eat these' — what it does say is, 'Eat these in small amounts.' But you can all breathe a sigh of relief at my next bit of news. Olive oil, once considered such a badie, does not raise blood cholesterol.

Finally, at the very tip, what do we find? Sugar. Sugar, that old-fashioned villain of dietary habits? You bet.

Now there are plenty of diet books around telling you to lay off the sugar, but while sugar isn't all that crash hot as a food, the Nutrition Foundation folk take the common-sense view — 'most people think that sugar makes food taste good and small amounts help to make the diet more enjoyable, which is very important.'

The thing I like about this pyramid is that it doesn't actually tell you to stop eating anything. Except salt. Salt has that Ghostbusters' sign right through it, meaning, 'Thou shalt not', but I'll go into that in more detail later. Now all of this is in line with what I plug throughout this book — eat what you like, but eat a balanced diet and don't overdo it.

Overdo it? Now eating lobster two or three times a week is overdoing it. I said earlier that I doubted that anyone eats lobster more than once or twice every couple of months, anyway. How could they afford to?

Well, I was putting this notion forward at a party recently when I found the one person who can afford, and does eat, lobster on a regular basis. Seems the bloke I was talking to has a relative at the Fish Markets from whom he buys his lobster wholesale, and he eats the rotten things four or five times a week. It's still expensive, but that's what he likes, so that's what he does.

I wasn't game to tell him so to his face (after all, if he lives long enough he may become a customer of mine and I don't want to upset customers, actual or potential), but I thought that would fall into my definition of overdoing it. That boy could end up with a cholesterol problem, not so much because he eats lobster, but because he eats it to excess. Lobster four or five times a week — and I speak as a professional seller of seafood — does not constitute a balanced diet.

The Healthy Diet Pyramid doesn't actually show a lobster — nor a prawn or a crab for that matter — but there is no specific warning against them, which suggests they are okay. But not four or five times a week.

It seems to me that if you follow the advice contained within the pyramid you'll live longer (unless you decide to tackle a 324 bus, of course) and I'm sure if you drop a line to the Australian Nutrition Foundation they'll send you a poster of the pyramid to hang in your kitchen.

That's basically it then. Let me just add that it is a good idea to stock up your fridge with the goodies that you know you can eat lots of, and make sure you've got lots of low-fat products in there as well. That could help you out during moments of temptation.

And I've a few words to say on that score, too. I go visiting my mum at least four times a week. Mum, as you may have gathered, is a terrific cook and she always has on offer such tempting delights as homemade cakes, Anzac biscuits, you name it. While I was losing weight I really had to psyche myself up to keep away from the goodies and just have a cup of tea, but Mum's Anzac biscuits are very difficult to resist, and sometimes, well, I proved all too human and fell by the wayside.

Now, there's a moral here for others who stray from the paths of righteousness while trying to knock off a few kilos. Don't worry. If you do slip up and give way to temptation, don't fret. It is *not* the end of the world, it is *not* something to overdramatise and to flail yourself about. Realise it has happened, take a deep breath, grit the teeth and try to do better next time. You're only human, after all — it's only the gods who are perfect. But don't go slipping too often — the only one you are cheating is yourself. The important thing is not to get too downhearted.

All things considered, it's not that bad, is it? And as you'll see when you look in the recipe section you can cook almost anything you want, even when you're combating a cholesterol problem.

Choosing Your Parents

So far we've been talking about cholesterol in relation to diet, but before we go any further we should take a slight detour and I'll tell you a little more about the cholesterol story. We all know the old saying about how to avoid going bald — choose hairy parents. It's beginning to look as though the same thing may apply to the subject in hand — there's some pretty strong opinion around to suggest that if you want to avoid cholesterol, make sure you pick parents who don't have a problem with it. Both of 'em.

In our family, Dad is as lean as a piece of string, fit as a flea and has the appetite of a horse — he can and will eat anything, my dad Jack. Anything.

Mother, on the other hand, should have been dead years ago and might well have been had she not had a pioneering operation by a visiting American specialist to remove a strip of affected artery leading to her brain. She was one of the patients on whom this American chose to demonstrate the technique, which had never been tried

40

The heredity question

in this country before.

The upshot of all this is that father's eat-anything genes and mother's 'maybe' cholesterol-prone genes have been equally divided among the children — two brothers took after Dad, two took after Mum. You know whom I took after.

Nowadays I can tease Mother that she was trying to kill us off when we were kids. She wasn't, of course; she was just a battling Aussie mum trying to do the best for her family.

In Mum we were blessed with a marvellous cook. All sorts of things might be going bad but she was determined we weren't going to starve, not the Doyle kids. Every day she would run up a big cream cake or chocolate sponge, and the highlight of the week was always the traditional roast lamb, with lashings of gravy and none of this modern notion of trimming the fat. Indeed, what fat we didn't eat went straight into a dripping bowl which we kids used to attack later in the week with a piece of bread whenever we felt peckish, and when we were kids that was just about all the time. How in the name of glory we didn't keel over dead from the effects of that dripping bowl alone, I'll never know.

Getting back to the heredity question, it's a bit like asking a group of economists for a prediction about the dollar. If you ask seven of them, you're likely to wind up with seven different answers. At least with the cholesterol and heredity link you'll only get one of five answers, no matter how many experts you ask: Yes, No, Maybe, Maybe Not, or Don't Know. The snag is you can get one of each of those answers from five different experts.

I mean, look at our house. Four brothers — two have to watch their cholesterol; two haven't a worry in the world. So is that heredity or not? Should I lay the blame for having to watch my cholesterol levels at Mum's genes or the dripping bowl? Or both? Or neither?

I reckon a bloke's got to use a bit of common sense and say the answer is Maybe. Now, that may sound a bit wishy washy, but it'll take a lot more statistical information than is around at the moment before I'm ready to blame my mum for anything, even if it is heredity.

And here let's think of our kids for a minute and use a bit more common sense. If you have to be careful about your cholesterol level, just bear in mind that this could be hereditary, therefore you may have passed it on to your kids. So don't start your kids off on today's equivalent of Mum's dripping bowl.

On the other hand, even if you don't have to think about your cholesterol problem, the problem may *not* be hereditary, in which case your kids could be prone anyway. So the same advice applies: keep 'em off the junk foods. Whether *you* have to watch your cholesterol levels or not, don't let your children start digging themselves an early grave.

A Salty Tale

Some years ago I read a novel about an Englishman's adventures at a farmhouse in post-war France. One episode stays in my mind...

The Englishman goes down for dinner on his first evening in the place. He sits down and when the dish is placed in front of him — it was coq au vin, as I recall — he reaches for the salt and proceeds to sprinkle it all over. The farmer's wife, proud of her cooking, is offended. 'Congratulations,' says she in the iciest of tones.

'Pardon?' The Englishman was clearly puzzled. 'Congratulations?'

'Certainement. M'sieur's palate is of the most exquisite, n'est-ce pas? It knows even without trying that there is not enough salt in the coq au vin. Quelle delicatesse.'

Oooer.

When I first read that book I felt sorry for the guy. I really cringed a little in sympathy with him in the face of madame's disapproval. Nowadays I find my approach has changed. I tend to find myself on madame's side.

'M'sieur's palate is of the most exquisite, n'est-ce pas?'

All of which brings us to the subject of salt. Now salt is not really directly connected to the cholesterol question, but it seems to be tied up with blood pressure and stroke and other nasties, so it is relevant when it comes to keeping you alive and enjoying life — and that after all is what this book is all about.

Let's start with a touch of controversy. Most medical authorities agree salt is not the best thing in the world — for certain people. There is an argument that susceptibility to high blood pressure is hereditary. But like the heredity factor in cholesterol, the jury is still out.

What tends to cloud the issue is the fact that our bodies need salt, or, to get a little more technical, sodium (salt simply happens to be the major source of sodium in our diet). So, just as our body needs some cholesterol, so it needs some sodium. Some sodium — not bloody great sprays of the stuff over everything.

There is research around that tells of two groups of Solomon Islanders who, as you'd expect, were racially identical. They enjoyed similar lifestyles and diets. But one mob cooked all its food in sea water and the other lot cooked in fresh water. The sea water lot had some cases of high blood pressure, or hypertension, and the fresh water lot were completely free of the disease. Note, the affected islanders had 'some' cases of hypertension. Not everyone went down with it.

In a society which has a high degree of sodium in its diet, and Australians are right in that category, it is reckoned that between 15 and 20 per cent of people are going to develop hypertension. Those aren't bad odds, I suppose, though one in five is enough to give me pause for thought. But what impresses me about that Solomon Island study is that none of the group which cooked in fresh water developed any form of high blood pressure. Not one. I know which odds I'd be playing.

The sneaky thing about salt is that you take it in ways you don't even think of. Sure, most sprinkle it on chips, some boil potatoes and vegetables in salt and we use 'salt to taste' in dozens of recipes. These are the obvious ways it can be absorbed. But we get it from lots of other foods, too. Ham, corned beef, smoked fish, salted crisps, butter... I tell you, it's a sodium minefield out there. I'll give you a list of suspects in a moment, but let me stress again, as I hope I have everywhere in this book: I am not telling you to stop eating any of these things. I am suggesting that you cut down on them.

As I also said earlier our body needs a little sodium, and we can get as much as needed from normal everyday foods such as meat, milk, eggs and vegetables in which sodium appears

48

naturally. Take those in conjunction with a whole heap of salt-laden foods and you can see there is no need at all to go adding it to food before or after it is cooked. No need, perhaps, but certainly for some a craving.

Some people, like our anecdotal Englishman, are mad for it. I've seen them at my restaurant, pouring it over everything in sight. I don't know that I would say it is addictive, but I do believe that we get a taste for it from early days and it stays with us as a very comforting psychological taste blanket.

So one thing to do for your children's sake is keep them away from too much salt before they develop the taste.

Cutting down on salt ain't easy for an adult, but like all other things in this book, it can be done. The most obvious way to start is to take the salt cellar off the lunch or dinner table, thus removing temptation, and stop putting it in whatever you are cooking. That's the cold turkey approach and good luck if you can do it. I recommend a gentler approach — cut down salt in cooking gradually and consciously use less salt from the salt cellar. Give yourself a couple of weeks to get over the shock to the system and notice, as time goes by, the subtle new flavours that start to come out of the food you cook. They have previously been masked by the salt. You

49

will suddenly realise it's a whole new world out there without soy sauce.

If your recipe calls for something like soy sauce — or anchovies or bacon or any of the foods on the list of suspects — then the smart thing to do is cut out salt entirely; there'll be more than enough in one of the salty ingredients.

One of the things the health pros suggest is that instead of using salt you flavour your dishes with herbs and other goodies. Some of my favourites are basil (especially on a beautiful fresh tomato), marjoram, sage, thyme and oregano. Spices are handy here — things like cardamom, cinnamon, cumin and nutmeg. And I'm not above using a drop of wine in casseroles, stews and desserts.

If that lot doesn't convince you that you can do without added salt, nothing will.

On the other hand, if you start to suffer withdrawal symptoms, try a salt substitute for a few weeks. It will hold you together between fixes, as it were, and you will slowly lose the desire for saltiness. Then all you have to do is kick the salt substitute.

THE USUAL GANG OF SUSPECTS

I'm not usually in favour of lists but I think it would help in your efforts to reduce your salt intake to know of the more villainous items on the salty scale. You can guess things like anchovies and soy sauce — they're so salty to taste they are prime suspects. But then consider these:

caviar
meat tenderisers and seasonings
bottled sauces and pickles
gravy powder and stock cubes
monosodium glutamate (good ol' MSG)
yeast extract (that means traditional Vegemite,
  I'm afraid) and meat extract
salami, ham and corned beef
parmesan and blue vein cheese
olives

They are the major culprits. Each of the items on that little shopping list comes with 2.5 per cent salt already in it. Talk to the health people and they will tell you that's very high.

The next list is hardly better. These foods have a salt content of between 1 and 2.5 per cent, and this is still high:

luncheon meats (like chicken roll, devon, garlic
  roll) pâté and liverwurst
frankfurts, pizza, fried takeaway foods, pies,
  sausages and hamburgers
canned and packet soups
canned sardines, tuna and salmon

crisps, cracker biscuits and bread (I repeat,
   bread — nothing is simple in this world)
margarine and hard cheese
many Chinese, Lebanese and Greek foods

Now that's the worst of it. You see, tinned
tuna is on that second list and, as I've told you,
I enjoy eating it. I don't overdose on the stuff,
much as I like it; I take it easy. You should do
the same — don't give up the olives because
they're on the loaded list; just don't eat them as
often as you are used to. Stop stuffing the caviar
down your throat seven nights — restrict yourself to five nights (I'm joking, I'm joking).

On the positive side you should look out for
all the foods that are coming on to the market
nowadays with reduced salt content. The
surprising thing is that many of the foods listed
as generally being high in salt, such as sauces
and crisps, for instance, also come in salt-reduced
varieties.

All of which means that the end of civilisa-
tion as we know it is not necessarily at hand.
There is life after reducing salt intake and if you're
one of those people susceptible to hypertension
it will probably be a lot happier life into the
bargain.

SUMMARY

• Your body needs some salt and it will probably be getting enough from your normal diet without having to add any.

• There seems to be a link between excess salt in the diet and hypertension, though even such people as the Australian Nutrition Foundation are very careful in saying their recommendations to eat less salt are based on 'evidence indicating that a reduction in salt intake may assist in the prevention of high blood pressure'.

• Don't try to cut out all salt from your diet — you won't be able to do it anyway. But do think about what you eat and do try to reduce your obvious intake through salt in cooking and sprinkled on food.

• High blood pressure combined with a cholesterol problem is not good news. Anything that can help get it down has to be the go.

• Realise that salt has a loaded, emotional background. The word 'salary' derives from salt money paid to soldiers hundreds of years ago; someone who is 'the salt of the earth' is a pretty good person; if you take salt with someone you are treated as a guest. Salt really is a part of our history. Just don't let your kids get hooked.

Don't Believe Everything They Tell You

There have been many things said and written on the subject of cholesterol and I am sure you will not be surprised to learn that not all of them are true. Meat, in particular beef, is only just recovering from the terrible beating it took in the media for a host of problems including a supposed link with cholesterol problems. Remember the headlines? Meat was going to give you dandruff and ingrown toenails before moving in for the kill with cancer and heart disease. It was all enough to make a bloke wonder how this country ever got going by living on mutton chops.

So how did meat come to take such a thrashing? Easy. It began in the United States (doesn't everything always seem to start in the United States?) when people, especially medical people, began to suspect that their meat wasn't all that crash hot for them. The headlines began to sprout over there and were soon picked up here. Meat was a killer, meat was fat-laden and horrible and you might as well do a Socrates and get stuck into the hemlock as eat a decent steak.

The story was also good for a book or two and when those authors came here to publicise their books, the message was always the same: meat can kill you.

But what no one woke up to was one basic fact: these Americans were talking about American meat, produced under American conditions to be eaten by American consumers. Their meat, for the most part, is heavily marbled (which is to say it has fat throughout the muscle area) and that is what causes the problems.

Australian meat, though, is quite different. If he were still with us you could ask Dr Pritikin himself. When this guru of the healthy diet advocated cutting down on meat intake he was talking in particular to an American audience about American meat. Did you know that he is on record as praising Australian meat for its nutritional qualities? Trust me. He did.

Australian beef is usually grass fed. Our cattle walk around paddocks all day, keeping themselves nice and lean, the way Australians like their beef.

To get back to the visiting American 'experts'... You can't really blame the journos for not asking that one question — 'What sort of meat are you talking about?' — because there was precious little information around. So they just took what the visitors said as gospel and out came the scare headlines.

Matters have improved. The Meat and Livestock Corporation has worked hard to overcome that particular misconception and the results are starting to show. Apart from all the advertising and so on, they run seminars for doctors to tell them the good news. Doctors? Sure. Do you know how many hours a medical student spends studying nutrition? It's not many, I can tell you, so your regular corner GP ain't necessarily a whizz-kid on nutrition, but they are getting better.

There has been another major improvement in communications. A couple of years ago, when all those scare headlines were flourishing, the only nutritional information we had on meat was a set of American and British tables — we were sort of working on the basis that what was true for the Poms and the Yanks was true for us and our meat. Wrong.

The Commonwealth Department of Health organised independent researchers to analyse meats for the revision of their food composition tables. This was the first time such research had been undertaken in forty years and — surprise, surprise — Australian meat was at last found not guilty. It should never have been on trial for its high fat content in the first place.

Just as well it was independent research. If the meaties had done it, how many people would have believed them? But the Commonwealth everyone could believe. And that's when the word really started to spread out — you can actually once again enjoy a barbecued steak (as long as you cook it properly, but that's another story) and you can look a sausage in the eye without seeing death at fifty paces.

I know how the meaties must have been feeling. I've already told you how fish and seafood have been seriously misrepresented in the cholesterol story. And even as we were starting work on this book Sydney papers were running daily stories about beach pollution and rivers being poisoned.

Being in the fishing industry, I can tell you the result of those stories was a disaster. Sydney people stopped buying fish almost overnight. Did it do any good to tell them most of the fish that is sold at the markets — and therefore in most fish shops and seafood restaurants around town — is caught more than 300 kilometres away from the pollution areas? Well, maybe it did, but the fact is that the scare headlines won the day, temporarily. And that was only the start of the misconceptions and inaccuracies in the reports.

So the moral of this story is a simple one:

take a lot of the things you read and hear in the media on nutritional matters with a grain of salt (metaphorically speaking, of course).

The Triglyceride Factor

Now back to that little problem that is probably facing a lot of us — weight. When my doc started putting the wind up me about my weight, it was a multi-pronged attack: there was another little foe I learnt about quite early in the piece. I was sitting across the desk from the doc one day when he pursed his lips and shook his head.

'Your triglycerides are up.'

I don't know about my triglycerides, but my eyebrows went up, I can tell you.

'So?' I said, trying to sound unconcerned, which wasn't so easy, as I had no idea what he was talking about. Fear of the unknown has quelled many a brave man.

'So that's the good news. We can get your triglycerides down. That's not the problem.'

'Okay,' I led with my chin, 'if that's the good news, what's the bad news?'

'Are you ready for this?'

'Doc,' I pleaded, 'spare me the dramatics, just tell me.'

'The bad news, I'm afraid, is that you've got

to cut down on the grog. Give it up, even.'

Give up the grog? Strewth, you could have knocked me down with a piece of four by two. Telling a bloke who enjoys the odd glass or two to give up the grog really isn't a very nice thing to do.

The doctor shrugged apologetically, but the sentence had been handed down. Was there no hope of an appeal somewhere? After all, I am fortunate enough to be able to produce my own drop of Hunter Valley plonk (fair dinkum) and I have a definite affinity for the happier products of the Barossa Valley and Western Australia, not to mention some particularly choice fortified numbers coming out of Victoria. Nor is the stuff that Mr Elliot and the like purvey to a discerning clientele exactly unknown to the Doyle palate, and the peaty delights of a single-malt whisky sometimes find me ready to renounce my Irish background and wish I could boast a Scottish lineage — that is until I get a sniff of Jamieson's Irish or a taste of a real Guinness. But, be that as it may, I think I can fairly say that my friends would describe me more as a connoisseur of these matters than a dedicated lush.

But, whatever my friends say, I can tell you that when the doc told me, 'Triglycerides up, grog down and maybe out,' your old mate Pete started thinking furiously.

First thought: 'If these triglycerides are such a problem, why the hell doesn't he hurry up and tell me what they are?' Second thought: 'If the doc says it's not such a problem to get them down, then if I hurry up and do that maybe I won't have to worry about the ban on grog.'

Now, logical as that may seem, it wasn't that simple. It never is that simple. Oscar Wilde got it right when he heard someone talking about 'the truth, pure and simple'. Oscar apparently put his hooter into high profile and said, 'My dear sir, the truth is never pure and rarely simple.' That might have been the other way around, but you get the general picture. Oscar Fingal O'Flahertie Wills, darlin' Irish boyo that he was, had it right.

Any'ow, as Hoges used to say, I started to look into this triglycerides business. The first thing to understand about triglycerides is that they are like armoured landing craft. You don't have to worry about them so much — it's the troops inside that are the cause for concern. In this case the troops we are talking about are globules of fat. That's what's going to come ashore from the landing craft and cause the devastation.

Now, there are three types of fat that concern us here — saturated, mono-unsaturated and poly-unsaturated. Don't bother about the names; they come from the chemical structure of each of them. The important thing to remember is that if you are trying to lose weight, you must cut down on all of them — saturated fats in particular. These are animal fats and, oddly enough, coconut and palm oil. Why coconut and palm oil? I don't know. I'm only a simple fisherman. What I do know is that you must cut down on all of them — saturated, mono and poly.

And before we go on, let me emphasise again: cut down, not out. You still need some fat in your diet.

So, triglycerides... They don't have as high a profile as cholesterol, so people aren't really as aware of them, but they are a heart risk factor (now, that's a bit of jargon for you — heart risk factor), so it's as well to look at them and fix them up while you're at it.

I have likened them to troop landing craft and that's not a bad analogy. They attract fats to themselves and move through the bloodstream, where the fat goes ashore and starts doing what damage it can. It seems to me to be nothing more than common sense to say that if you can reduce the number of triglycerides in your bloodstream (that is, the number of fat carriers), then you will reduce the amount of fat.

The snag is that the Minister for Fear and Despondency whom I laughingly call my medical adviser was on the right track when he told me to lay off the grog. Grog is one of the things that has a direct effect on the amount of triglycerides dropping off all those fatty invaders in your bloodstream — the more grog you drink, the more triglycerides. But in my case, I'm happy to say the picture didn't turn out to be entirely bleak. The doc did advise cutting out the grog entirely, but I managed to knock the problem by cutting down. I was careful about amounts. I'm not a big beer man, but on a hot day there's nothing to match a chilly, beaded stubby. But — one or two at most will do me fine.

Jeanie, my wife, doesn't drink, so if we are home dining alone, as happens once every three or four months, it seems, I'll have a scotch or two. If we have friends around, I'll open a bottle or three of wine.

One thing I don't do is drink cask wine. I don't think I am a snob about this, but I don't like the stuff. I'd rather go without for two or three days, save up and buy a decent drop that I really enjoy. Maybe that attitude helped while I was trying to get down to my fighting weight. And I do know that the odd day or two off the grog didn't harm the cause, either.

It's a bit more of what I've been preaching all the way through, really — don't walk around in fear and trembling of the preachings of every damned food crank and nutrition nut. Take it easy, do all the things in moderation and you can still enjoy the good things in life. Maybe they will be a little more spaced out than previously, but you can still have them and still be alive to enjoy them.

And that truly is the benefit of looking after yourself. Isn't it?

That was another thing the doc told me about reducing triglycerides. 'If you can reduce the weight,' he said with a nasty laugh, 'get rid of some more of that flab, that will help you get your triglycerides down.'

So there we are, back to the old weight problem. I've already told you about the sensible eating programme I adopted; perhaps now it's time to give you a few more clues about battling the enemy.

A Little Bit of Exercise Never Hurt Anyone

That's right, you read the heading correctly — exercise. When I first started to tackle my burgeoning weight problem I tried to avoid the subject, thought that it would be easier just to stop eating. After all, just ask those political jokers who try to reform the world by going on a starvation diet: stop eating and the pounds, or their modern equivalents the kilograms, will fall away.

Alas, nothing is that simple. It may be a bit obvious to say this, but our body needs food to keep going. Food provides the kilojoules we need to enable us to do all sorts of things. But then if we don't *do* all sorts of things, the food tends to sit in the body and build up fat. The trick, then, is to have the body do something to burn up the kilojoules so they cannot be translated into kilograms on the midriff.

So, yes, the answer was starting to come up as exercise. Exercise? At my age? Okay, okay, while I'm not exactly in the first flush of youth,

I'm not exactly over the hill, either. But still, exercise didn't really sound like my go. I'm not one to don sweat suit and Reeboks, throw a sweatband around my forehead and charge around the streets frightening old ladies and horses, so jogging is out.

The prospect of sitting still while cycling hundreds of kilometres to nowhere on one of these stationary bikes did not grab me nor did the notion of sitting in comfort and pushing chunks of iron up and down in some fancy fitness centre (aka a gym).

I decided that I'd try a tentative one on my doc. 'What about,' I began almost shamefaced, 'what about if I took up, say, er, walking?'

He looked at me in some amazement and I thought for a moment he was going to burst out laughing and tell me I had to swim four kilometres a day, jog for an hour, play tennis three times a week and generally behave like an ironman trying to win a cornflakes contract.

'Walking,' said the doc. 'At your age I wouldn't suggest anything else.' I ignored the crack about my age. 'Walking is exactly what you should be doing. Nothing too strenuous, no twenty kilometre hikes before breakfast. Just take ten minutes at a time, a couple of times a day and build up to a total of thirty minutes a day, not necessarily all in one hit...'

Oh wise practitioner, a very Solomon among witch doctors. A couple of ten minute walks sounded very much more like my idea of exercise. Nowadays I have even managed to slot my exercise into my working day.

Take lunch, for instance. One way and another I find myself at a business lunch most days of the week — and how to deal with those is another story. Once upon a time I would drive into town or wherever, head for the nearest car park, leave the car and then pay some corporate extortionist a grossly inflated fee just to have my car sit somewhere nearby for a couple of hours. Not anymore. Nowadays I drive to within a kilometre or so of where I want to go, find a parking spot easily and then I walk. At the end of the lunch I walk back to the car. A couple of Ks? Ten to twenty minutes each way? Exercise. Dead easy.

This means I don't insult my hosts by not eating; it also means that after lunch I can walk off any surplus kilojoules that may have slipped my guard.

If I don't get my few minutes walk at lunchtime, I grab a few minutes in the evening or some other time, but I do it. That's the important thing. I do it and I do it regularly. I'm not into all this sweaty jockstrap stuff, a pox on the iron pumpers, say I (and I wouldn't give you twopence for the favours of these women who go in for body building and end up looking like miniature Arnold Schwartzneggers). No a daily walk is the go — provided it is daily.

And it's so easy to do for yourself. Get up fifteen minutes earlier and go for a walk around the block; better still, if the newsagency isn't too far away, cancel your morning delivery and walk to get the papers in the mornings. The same thing when you have to nick up to the local milk bar; don't jump into the car — use your feet to get there. That's all it takes to get that regular daily exercise. And even if you don't drive, try getting off your bus or train (or tram) a couple of stops or a station earlier. The walk itself won't have you jumping out of your skin ready to leap into the ring and murder Mike Tyson or skin Rambo with a blunt shearer's cook's knife, but it will get you burning up those kilojoules, and that, you can be assured, will help lose that weight.

Once you've got a daily schedule going, you'll actually come to enjoy it. You'd be surprised what you see when you go walking, things you never glimpse behind the wheel of a car or a seat in the train.

I'm not saying here that you shouldn't do all those exercise things I'm not happy with. Go for your life is my attitude. It's your life. If you want to smell like a sweathog or look like Mrs Atlas, that's your prerogative. Just count me out. I'm going for a walk, thank you. See you when I get back.

Business Lunches Are Still on the Menu

You probably groan at the thought of trying to juggle a business lunch at the same time as keeping an eye on your cholesterol level. I must say that some of the business lunches of my experience — one-third of a chook, twenty-two peas, two potatoes and three miserable carrots — wouldn't do much major damage to a bloke looking after his weight. Yes, well, I will admit that there have been others of a more heavyweight nature. But it can be quite simple really.

Most restaurants have salads of some description on the menu and unless you choose one consisting almost solely of creamy cheeses these are usually pretty safe as an entree. They also help fill you up, so it's not a bad idea to have one with whatever you choose as a main course. If salad doesn't inspire you as an entree, find out what the soup of the day is, but be sensible about it and if it is obviously loaded with cream or similar goodies give it a miss this time. If bread

71

is served prior to the entree you can help yourself to some of that — and if you can't enjoy it
without butter, just remember to be very spar-
ing. And when I say bread, I don't mean garlic
or herb bread, which is often swimming in a sea
of butter. I think you'll agree that is pushing things
too far.

Getting on to the main course, it's always safest
to choose something that is grilled — and avoid
anything with sauces or that's going to be
smothered in cheese. As I mentioned when giving you my sensible eating plan, you don't have
to exclude pasta from the menu — just make sure
that the one you choose isn't laden with cream
or fatty foods. You know that this is all common
sense really, don't you? It's not really that hard
at all.

Oh, and another hint. Drink lots of water.
It is a good way of keeping the appetite down
and so reducing the likelihood of straying onto
the paths of temptation. And if you've constant-
ly got a glass of water in front of you, as long
as you're drinking something nobody really no-
tices what it is and you can avoid being pressed
to drink glass after glass of wine.

When it comes to desserts, there is nothing
nicer and more refreshing than a fresh fruit salad,
so that is a simple matter really. And you may
also find other fruit dishes that are not swamped

with fattening extras on the menu as well.

But do remembr that if you slip up somewhere along the line, don't get too despondent. Just tell yourself you'll do better next time, and make sure you put quite a bit of distance between this slip up and the next one. You can't expect it to be smooth sailing all the way, can you?

Up, Up and Away

Well, I've just about said my piece now, but before I leave you to embark on a little of what you fancy, I'll just relate a little tale.

I'm a peacable sort of character generally speaking, but I must say I arrived in Sydney after a flight from Perth recently and I was fit to be tied.

It had been a meal flight (well, they all are between Perth and Sydney, aren't they?) and everything they served I had to reject. Everything. Well, almost everything. I managed to force down a bit of salad and a fruit juice.

I have to confess I gave my friends a bad time about airlines in general, and it had nothing to do with the pilots' dispute. I contrasted my treatment on a major route flight with what I'd received on the earlier connecting flight from Broome to Perth. That had been a meal flight, too, but on that flight I had been able to eat all they put in front of me.

'This Western Australian Airlines is the shot,' I told my friends. 'A little state airline and they

74

can do the right thing. Then you get on board the big boys' airlines and what happens? They try to kill a bloke with what they give you to eat.'

Okay, this may have been me doing a bit of overreacting, but anyone who has suffered a long plane trip knows what I am on about.

Then along comes my co-pilot, Taffy. 'Pete,' he says, 'you've got it wrong. Did you ring the airline and tell them that you wanted a meal suitable for a bloke with cholesterol?'

No. In a word. I hadn't. The thought hadn't even occurred to me.

'Right,' says Taffy. 'We're not putting the blast on airlines until we check it out.'

Taffy checked it out. Rang Ansett and talked to a fellow in Melbourne name of Jock Balding and Jock gave Taffy the word (it's beginning to sound like old Brits' week, isn't it? All we need now is a Paddy and a Pom and we'll boot home a four-horse accumulator...but I digress). Jock assured Taffy that all you do is tell the person who takes your booking that you are keeping an eye on your cholesterol levels and Ansett will arrange a special meal for you — that's provided you're on a flight on which you would normally be served a meal.

Breakfast on Ansett will consist of:
Grilled fillet steak
Grilled tomato

Wholemeal roll
Margarine and honey
Fresh fruit
Orange juice
Now that's not all bad.

You get the same sort of treatment on Australian Airlines. Tell them when you're booking that if they're serving a meal you would like them to take into account that you have a cholesterol problem and they'll do the right thing. Here's what you'll get for dinner:

Chicken breast (without the skin, please note)
Steamed vegetables
Sauce (made from the chicken stock and containing no butter or cream)
Salad
Fresh fruit

And that doesn't sound too bad, either.

Taffy used to do some work for an airline, so he knows about these things. He tells me special meals are a bit of a pain for the airlines because they have to match the meal to a particular seat in an aircraft where the passenger is sitting and in logistical terms this can be tricky. But they do it and it's all part of the service, so don't fret about mucking up your cholesterol when next you fly.

SUMMARY

Don't do as I did, do as I say. I didn't realise the airlines had such a service for people keeping a beady eye on their cholesterol level. Kosher I knew about, vegetarian, diabetic...but, yes, they have a special diet for people like you and me. You are the paying passenger. Ask and ye shall receive — provided you ask in time and they can overcome the logistical problems of finding you in the aircraft. (And they usually can, says Taffy.)

Pete's Personal PS: I have just come back from a trip to the United States. Lucky me. But at this point I am giving co-pilot Taffy the flick and having my unabashed say about cholesterol meals on international flights. By and large they're a bloody disaster. They all seem to offer you fish and fish doesn't travel well, it just collapses. The only exception I have found is Air New Zealand and then only when the flight is coming out of New Zealand. They've got their own fish there and they do it very well.

When I was going to America on this trip — I'd better not tell you which airline I was flying with or they'll sue me — I bloody near starved to death, survived on three beans, two potatoes

78

and a crust. That was the main meal. Breakfast was croissants, muffins, butter and cream and all that stuff — no good for someone looking after cholesterol levels, so you can forget about that. But there was fruit. I ate the fruit. Fruit's good for you on a flight; it makes the bowels work like buggery.

And as for the meals on internal American flights — well, at one stage I thought, to hell with it, I'll catch everything the locals have got; I'll have a normal meal. Big mistake. That particular meal consisted of two packets of peanuts and an oatmeal bar with a ton of cholesterol in it. Make that a ton and a half.

Those Americans sure have a sweet tooth.

The moral of all this, I suppose, is that while I'd better dip me lid to our Aussie airlines (or Taffy will give me a hard time), I'm not too happy about American internal airlines and I'm definitely not too happy about international airlines.

So You Want To Know About a Millimole?

Wherever I go in this country, from Broome to Broken Hill, from Thornleigh to Thursday Island, there is one question keeps cropping up. You can settle down for a cooling couple in a Darwin beer garden or a post-prandial port in a Perth pub and there's always some joker who will come up to you and ask: 'What is a millimole?'

That's the question, so help me. What is a millimole?

Well, I'll tell you. A millimole is a unit of measurement to indicate how much cholesterol you have in every litre of blood. It's that mysterious figure the quack uses when he says, 'Your count is seven — you've got to get it down.'

What he means is that in every litre of blood you have seven millimoles of cholesterol.

The word itself comes from 'milli' (as in millimetre, and meaning thousand or a thousandth part) and 'molecule'.

Now, your doctor will tell you that a count

of five (that is, five millimoles of cholesterol in every litre of blood) is about average. (The National Heart Foundation gives a figure of 5.5 millimoles per litre as desirable, but the lower the better.) Now that's not a very high figure at all — you can achieve that without even trying, and in fact most people do, which is why it is the average figure. A decimal point or two more than that isn't going to kill you, but once you start nudging up above the six mark then storm warning signals should be hoisted. Hit seven and you should start taking definite steps to bring it down.

I should know. My count got to nine and in the words of my Western Australian mate Michael Kailis, 'You should have been dead, you bugger.'

Well, I'm not. I'm alive to tell the tale, my count is down to five and I'm going to keep it there, thank you very much.

RECIPES

You may have gathered by now that Pete likes his tucker, anything from a good old fashioned baked dinner (lamb and mint sauce, three vegies — smashing) to the most delicate of seafood salads. Love it. All of it. And I'm still eating all of it and enjoying it. If you think watching what you eat is dull, you'd better look through these recipes and learn the truth — you can still eat like an emperor without having to give up flavour and taste and eye appeal and all the rest of the good things about food.

Just to whet your appetite, as it were, I'm giving you a list of what's coming up. I don't think you'll find this lot dull and boring.

Dips and Appetisers
Herbed cheese dip
Mexican bean dip
Chicken nibbles

Soups
Quick tomato and basil soup
Belgian pumpkin soup
Pumpkin and lentil soup
Cream of snapper soup

Chicken
Hot chili chicken
Microwave roasted chicken
Nutty orange drumsticks

Fish
Microwave tropical fish
Tuna with Provençale sauce
Doyle's poached, grilled and barbecued fish
Fish curry
Microwave baked cod

Meat
Veal asparagus rolls
Veal with rice
Veal shanks
Glazed pork kebabs
Mexican pork
Barbecued fillets of lamb
Drunken roast lamb
Lamb and lentils

Lamb stew and dumplings
Meatball medley
Stir fried beef
French pot roast
Beef and potato curry

Pasta
Meat sauce
Neapolitan tomato sauce
Tomato sauce with marsala
Microwave spinach and pine nut sauce
Mussel sauce

Largely Vegetarian
Microwave curried vegetables
Stuffed tomatoes
Baked aubergines with tomatoes

Sweets
Fruit jelly with mint cream
Apple and mango jelly
Sherried peaches
Fresh fruit compote
Melon and raspberry compote
Microwave quick Christmas pudding

Most recipes here can be adapted either for the microwave or ordinary stoves. The specific microwave recipes are for an average 650-watt model. Please check with your microwave instruction book.

Hints

• Remember there are some pretty flash recipe books to be had from the National Heart Foundation (look up your telephone directory for the local state division), and also from your local state Fish Marketing Authority and from the Australian Meat and Live-stock Corporation, Box 4129, GPO Sydney 2001 or phone (02) 260 3111.

• Instead of using oil to brown meat and vegetables, a little stock (preferably homemade) in a non-stick pan over a medium to low heat, will work just as well. If you do use an oil make it pure olive oil or grapeseed.

• Vegetables and fish are easily cooked in a microwave without any fat coming near them. Fish is especially good done in a microwave.

Dips and Appetisers

Many dips can be made by using low-fat yoghurt or cottage cheese mixed with curry, herbs, onion or garlic and served with sliced mushrooms, celery, carrot or any other vegetable sticks, cauliflower florets, broccoli and radishes.

Herbed cheese dip

1 cup cottage cheese
½ teaspoon each dried rosemary and dried thyme
1 clove garlic, peeled and crushed
2 tablespoons chopped parsley
2 finely chopped shallots

Mix together and serve with raw vegetable pieces.

Mexican bean dip

250 g canned kidney beans, drained
2 cloves garlic, crushed
¼ teaspoon tabasco
2 teaspoons ground cumin
1 tablespoon tomato paste, no added salt
1 tablespoon yoghurt
juice of ½ lemon
1 teaspoon chopped chives or shallots

Rinse the beans under running water. Mix all ingredients together, except for the chives/shallots, and blend until smooth. Sprinkle with chives/shallots and serve with raw vegetables.

Chicken nibbles

1½ tablespoons olive or grapeseed oil
1 egg white, slightly beaten
2 tablespoons lemon juice
2 large whole chicken breasts (skin and fat
* removed)*
1 teaspoon powdered rosemary
3 cloves garlic, peeled and crushed
½ cup fine bread crumbs

Mix together oil, egg white and lemon juice. Cut
each breast into small pieces (about 16). Combine
the bread crumbs, salt, rosemary and garlic on a
plate. Dip the chicken into the lemon mixture then
roll in the bread crumbs. Place the pieces on a
greased baking dish in one layer and bake for
10–15 minutes in a moderate oven, until golden.

Soups

Quick tomato and basil soup
(Serves 4)

2 medium green apples
1½ cups chicken stock
1 can (440 g) peeled tomatoes, no added salt,
   or 3 or 4 peeled fresh tomatoes
½ cup chopped fresh basil
pepper

Peel apples and cook in the chicken stock until
soft. Combine apples, stock, tomatoes, pepper
and basil and blend. Chill and serve with
crushed ice and extra basil.

Belgian pumpkin soup

(Serves 6)

3 cups pumpkin purée
4 cups chicken stock
1 onion, thickly sliced
4 whole cloves
pepper
1 bay leaf
1 cup low-fat milk
1½ tablespoons Worcestershire sauce
chopped parsley to garnish

Combine pumpkin, chicken stock, onion, cloves, pepper and bay leaf and simmer for half an hour. Remove cloves and bay leaf and add milk and Worcestershire sauce. Reheat and serve with chopped parsley.

Pumpkin and lentil soup

(Serves 6)

2 cups sliced pumpkin
½ cup washed red lentils (discard the dark ones)
1 chopped onion
1 litre chicken stock
chopped parsley to garnish

Mix all ingredients together and cook for
45 minutes. Pureé in blender and reheat.
Serve with chopped parsley.

Cream of snapper soup

(Serves 8)

8 cups of fish stock
2 large whole potatoes, peeled
2 large brown onions, chopped finely
4 stalks celery, chopped finely
½ cup rice or sago
1 teaspoon basil
4 drops tabasco sauce
1–2 bay leaves, to taste
seasoning to taste
¼ cup plain flour
1 cup low-fat milk
2 teaspoons curry powder
2 or 3 large carrots, grated
2 teaspoons tomato paste, no added salt
chopped parsley

Heat the fish stock, then add the potatoes,
onions, celery, rice, basil, tabasco, bay leaves and
seasoning. Cook for ½ hour. Mix the plain flour
to a smooth paste with the cup of milk and thicken
soup mixture. Add the curry powder. Let the flour
cook through the mixture until you cannot taste it.
Add tomato paste, stir well and a few minutes
before the soup is ready, put in the grated carrot.
Garnish with parsley and serve with sippets
of dry toast.

Chicken

Hot chili chicken
(Serves 4)

*750 g chicken, boned, skinned and cleaned of
   fat*
2 medium–large onions, chopped
2 small red chilies, chopped
*1½ tablespoons grapeseed or olive oil or,
   if using a non-stick pan, 2 tablespoons stock*
½ teaspoon ground cumin
½ teaspoon ground ginger
*½–1 cup chicken stock (made from bones of
   chicken)*
2 tablespoons low-salt soy sauce
3 tablespoons wine or cider vinegar

Fry onion and chilies in the oil (or stock) until
onions are clear. Add spices and stir until well
blended (about 1 minute). Add chicken and
stock and simmer, covered, for 15 minutes.
Add soy sauce and vinegar. Turn heat to
medium, stir and cook a further 25 minutes.
Serve over steamed rice.

Microwave roasted chicken*

(Serves 4)

1 No. 15 chicken (1½ kg), skinned and with fat
   removed
3 tablespoons low-salt soy sauce
1 tablespoon lemon juice
1 tablespoon dry sherry
½ teaspoon sesame oil
1 clove garlic, crushed
½ teaspoon ground ginger
1 tablespoon honey

Mix the soy, lemon juice, sherry, oil, garlic, ginger
and honey and brush over the chicken. Leave for
at least one hour. Place chicken, breast down, on a
microwave rack. Cover with microwave bake
paper and cook for 15 minutes at 70 per cent
power. Turn the chicken, baste and cook for
further 15 minutes. Wrap chicken in foil and rest it
for 10 minutes before serving.

* This dish may be cooked in an ordinary
convection oven. Place chicken in a casserole
dish with a lid so as not to dry it out, and cook for
approximately one hour, turning the chicken
halfway through the cooking.

Nutty orange drumsticks

(Serves 6)

1½–2 kg chicken drumsticks, skin removed
180 ml fresh orange juice
½ cup chicken stock
½ teaspoon dry mustard
1 teaspoon curry powder
2 tablespoons cornflour or arrowroot
¼ cup water
½ cup finely chopped shallots
½ cup chopped walnuts or almonds

Combine orange juice, stock, mustard and curry powder in a jug to make a sauce. Arrange drumsticks in roasting dish and pour sauce over chicken. Cover and cook in a moderate oven until chicken is tender. Remove drumsticks to serving platter. Combine the cornflour or arrowroot with the water and blend into remaining sauce. Add shallots and nuts and cook, stirring, until thickened. Pour sauce over chicken.

Note: This recipe may also be made using salmon fillets.

Fish

Microwave tropical fish
(Serves 2)

250 g fish fillets — any white fish will do
2 tablespoons chopped chives
¼ to ½ cup pineapple juice
¼ cup chopped avocado
sprinkle of lemon pepper
¼ cup finely chopped zucchini
2 teaspoons polyunsaturated margarine

Melt the margarine in a shallow microwave dish. Place fish in margarine. Add remaining ingredients, cover and cook in microwave for 4 minutes at 80 per cent power.

Tuna with Provençale sauce

(Serves 4)

4 tuna steaks
½ cup white wine
juice of ½ lemon
freshly ground black pepper
2 teaspoons olive oil
2 cloves garlic
1 medium onion, chopped
1 green pepper, chopped, blanched and sliced
2 shallots, chopped
½ cup fish stock
3 large tomatoes, skinned, chopped and seeded,
*   or 1 can (440 g) tomatoes, no added salt*
chopped parsley

Place tuna in a bowl. Combine wine, lemon juice, pepper and half the olive oil. Pour over fish and marinate for at least 2 hours. When ready, heat rest of the oil in a pan and fry garlic and onion until the onion is golden. Add the green pepper and shake over the heat for a few minutes. Turn out and keep warm. Drain the fish, reserving the marinade. Cook in hot non-stick pan or under a hot grill or on charcoal grill, for about 10 minutes, turning once. Remove, place with onions, pepper and garlic and keep warm. Place the shallots, stock, tomatoes and marinade in pan and bring to the boil. Pour over tuna. Garnish with the chopped parsley and serve with boiled new potatoes.

Doyle's method for poached, grilled and barbecued fish

The following recipes have been ever so slightly adapted from my mother's popular book, *The Doyle's Fish Cookbook*. (Thank you, mother. It's times like this a bloke realises a mother is a boy's best friend.)

Poached

Place fish fillets or steaks in a pan with enough water to cover them. Add a little chopped onion and celery, a few peppercorns, a bay leaf, a pinch of basil and about 1 tablespoon tarragon vinegar or brown vinegar.

Cover with lid, bring to the boil, reduce heat to low and simmer slowly for 10 to 15 minutes, depending on thickness of fish. Test if fish is cooked with a fork; if it flakes easily it is done.

Remove fish from liquid with a spatula and place on hot plates. Reserve stock for use in other recipes or to make a sauce for the fish. Serve garnished with lemon wedges and chopped parsley.

Grilled

Place the fish in a shallow pan, with a little water and a touch of polyunsaturated margarine. For whole fish, make two shallow cuts on each side.

Brush the fish with a little olive oil, pop it under a hot griller, reduce heat slightly, and baste again as it is cooking. Cooking time depends on the thickness of the fish — 10 to 15 minutes for thick fillets; for whole fish, 10 to 15 minutes each side.

When ready place the fish on a very hot serving plate and serve with lemon and chopped parsley. Serve a nice sauce with your grilled fish (e.g. mushroom) to correct any dryness.

Barbecued

(Serves 4)

2 kg fish fillets or whole fish, cleaned
1 large brown onion, sliced
1 green or red capsicum, sliced
freshly ground black pepper
juice of ½ lemon
2 tablespoons olive oil
tabasco sauce
1 large can tomatoes, no added salt

Place the fish on greased aluminium foil,
supported, if you like, in an old baking dish.
Put the onion and capsicum over the fish. Add the
pepper and lemon juice, and the oil and tabasco
sauce to taste. Pour the tomatoes carefully over the
top.

Cover with more greased foil and crimp edges
to hold in the liquid from the tomatoes. Place over
a low charcoal fire; let cook for about 20 minutes.
If fish is large, make a small hole in top layer of foil
and continue cooking until the fish is tender.
Otherwise serve immediately.

Curried fish

(Serves 4–5)

1 *tablespoon olive oil or polyunsaturated margarine*
1 *kg flathead (or cod, gemfish etc) washed, dried, skinned and boned, and cut into chunks*
1 *medium brown onion, sliced*
2 *teaspoons curry powder*
1 *tablespoon plain flour*
2 *cups fish stock*
1 *tablespoon lemon juice*
cayenne pepper
seasonings

Melt the margarine or oil in a saucepan and fry fish lightly for a few minutes. Take out and set aside. Put onion, curry powder and flour in the pan. Cook slowly for about 15 minutes. Do not let the onion get too brown.

Add stock, stir until it boils and then simmer 20 minutes. Add lemon juice, a sprinkle of cayenne pepper and seasonings to taste.

Add fish very, very slowly. On a low flame, cook for 30 minutes so that the fish absorbs the curry flavour. Make sure you put a tight-fitting lid over the saucepan. Stir occasionally so the fish does not stick to the bottom and burn.

Serve with boiled rice and lemon wedges.

Microwave baked cod

(Serves 4)

1 kg fresh cod or haddock
juice of 2 lemons
2 oranges, sliced
2 tomatoes, sliced
2 onions, sliced
250 g mushrooms
½ teaspoon paprika
½ teaspoon thyme
¼ teaspoon freshly ground black pepper
3 tablespoons dry white wine
lemon wedges

Into a glass baking dish, place fish which has been freshly washed and patted dry with paper towel. Squeeze lemon juice over fish. Arrange alternate slices of oranges and tomatoes over top of fish, then spread onion rings on top again. Arrange remainder of onions and the mushrooms around the sides of fish.

Sprinkle seasonings over fish and surrounding ingredients. Sprinkle wine over all ingredients. Cook 5–7 minutes on high setting of microwave, remove from oven and let stand covered for 3 minutes. Alternatively, cook in ordinary moderate oven for about 30 minutes. Serve with fluffy rice and lemon wedges.

Meat

VEAL

Veal asparagus rolls
(Serves 6)

6 large veal steaks
2 tablespoons lemon juice
2 tablespoons grated Parmesan cheese
1 × 340 g can asparagus spears, no added
  salt, drained (liquid reserved)
black pepper
2 teaspoons olive or grapeseed oil
1 small carton low-fat yoghurt
½ cup white wine
toothpicks (not for eating, but to keep the rolls
  together — just in case you were wondering)

Pound veal steaks. Sprinkle each with lemon
juice and Parmesan cheese. Top each with 2–3
asparagus spears. Season to taste with pepper.
Roll up and secure with toothpicks.

Heat oil in large frying pan. Fry veal rolls 8–10 minutes until browned, turning occasionally. Remove and drain. Pour reserved asparagus liquid, yoghurt and wine into pan. Bring to boil, return veal, and simmer until heated through. Serve with boiled noodles and steamed or microwaved carrots and broccoli.

Veal with rice

(Serves 4–5)

750 g veal, cut in cubes
1 tablespoon olive oil or, if using non-stick
*   pan, 2 tablespoons veal or chicken stock*
1 onion, chopped
3–4 large ripe tomatoes, peeled, seeded and
*   coarsely chopped*
1 tablespoon flour
2 cups veal or chicken stock
1 cup water or white wine
1 clove garlic, crushed
pepper
12 mushrooms

In a heavy pot, brown the veal in the hot oil or 2 tablespoons stock. Add the onion and tomatoes and brown lightly. Sprinkle the mixture with the flour and gradually stir in the stock and the water or wine. Add the garlic and pepper to taste. Cover the pot and simmer the meat over low heat for 1 hour until it is tender. Add the mushrooms to the pot 15 minutes before the meat is done. Serve over steamed rice.

Veal shanks

(Serves 4)

4 veal shanks (have butcher split them)
3 tablespoons plain flour, seasoned
2 teaspoons polyunsaturated oil
2 brown onions, chopped
1 cup brown stock
1 can tomato purée, no added salt
zest from a lemon
1 bay leaf
pepper to taste
½ cup low-fat milk
½ cup cottage cheese
2 teaspoons cornflour (optional)

Trim fat from the shanks and dust with
seasoned flour and brown in a little oil in a
frying pan. Remove to a roasting pan. Fry the
onions in the remaining oil and add them to
the roasting pan. Add the stock, tomato purée,
lemon zest, bay leaf and pepper. Cover the
pan and braise the shanks in a moderate oven
for about 2 hours. Strain the juices into a
saucepan, skim off any fat and reduce juices to
2 cups. Add the milk and cheese. If desired,
thicken the sauce with the cornflour mixed
with a little water. Pour the sauce over the
shanks in the pan and reheat. Serve with
sweet and sour red cabbage and noodles.

PORK

Glazed pork kebabs

(Serves 4)

750 g pork fillet, trimmed of fat and cut into
  cubes
1 tablespoon honey
1 tablespoon instant coffee powder
2 teaspoons lemon juice
2 cloves garlic, crushed
1 red capsicum and 1 green capsicum, coarsely
  chopped
1 small onion, quartered and segmented
8 button mushrooms

Marinate meat in combined honey, coffee, lemon
juice and garlic for 10 minutes.
Thread meat and vegetables on to water-soaked
bamboo skewers and grill on high heat 4–6
minutes each side. Serve on steamed brown rice
with a salad.

Mexican pork

(Serves 4)

750 g lean pork, cut into cubes
1 tablespoon oil or, if using a non-stick pan,
  2 tablespoons stock
1 large onion
1 cooking apple
2 tablespoons flour
1 teaspoon low-salt soy sauce
1 cup chicken stock
1 red capsicum and 1 green capsicum, diced
1 clove garlic, crushed
2 teaspoons sugar
1½ teaspoons chili powder
seasoning to taste

Peel and chop onion and apple, and place with pork in oil (or stock) in large saucepan. When pork is browned on all sides, remove pork, onion, and apple from pan. Add flour to juices in pan and mix well. Stir in sufficient stock to make a smooth thin sauce and continue stirring until it boils. Add capsicums, garlic, sugar, chili powder, seasoning, soy sauce and the pork, onion and apple. Add the remainder of the stock (add water if needed) to cover and simmer for 1 hour, until tender. Serve with steamed spiced cabbage and noodles.

LAMB

Barbecued fillets of lamb
(Serves 3–4)

2 fillets of lamb (trimmed of all fat)
1 teaspoon dried rosemary
½ teaspoon dried thyme
2 teaspoons chopped fresh mint (or ½
*   teaspoon dried mint)*
3 cm of ginger, freshly grated
2 cloves garlic, crushed
1 teaspoon olive oil
2 tablespoons low-salt soy sauce
½ teaspoon dried thyme
4 shallots, finely chopped

Make a paste of the herbs, ginger, garlic, oil, soy and shallots and spread over the lamb. Leave for approximately 2 hours and grill for 2 to 3 minutes on either side. Serve with jacket potatoes and salad. Can also be cooked in a hot pan.

Drunken roast lamb

(Serves 6)

1 leg of lamb, 1½–2 kg
2–3 cloves garlic, sliced
½ cup white wine
½ cup orange juice
ground thyme
brown stock
2½ teaspoons cornflour

Trim the leg and pierce the flesh on the fleshy side to allow you to insert pieces of the sliced garlic. Rub with the thyme and place the leg on a rack in an oven dish. Pour the wine and orange juice over it and leave to marinate for about 2 hours. Cook lamb, using marinade as a baste, in a moderate oven for about 1½ hours. Place lamb aside and leave for about 15 minutes before carving.

For gravy, skim fat from pan juices (it helps if you put pan in a freezer for a few minutes). Add enough stock to make about 2 cups of liquid. Stir in cornflour blended with a little water. Bring to boil, stirring occasionally until thickened. Serve with vegetables and mint sauce.

To cook the lamb in a microwave, shield shank end with foil. Microwave on high for 10 minutes then reduce power to medium (70 per cent) and

grams. Halfway through cooking, remove the foil and turn the lamb. When cooked, wrap the lamb in foil and let it rest for 15 minutes.

Lamb and lentils

(Serves 4)

4 lamb shanks (or 8 best-end neck chops),
  trim off fat
1 onion, chopped
1½ cups washed brown or green lentils
stock or boiling water
½ teaspoon dried thyme
1 bay leaf
seasoning to taste
chopped parsley

Place shanks and onion in large non-stick pot,
brown on low heat. Add lentils, herbs and
seasoning. Cover with stock or boiling water
and simmer 1½ hours. Cool and skim off fat.
Reheat. Place in a large dish and serve
sprinkled with parsley.

Lamb stew and dumplings

(Serves 4)

*500 g of **very lean** lamb, cubed, or neck chops*
*   with fat removed*
2 medium onions, sliced
2 cups stock
4 medium carrots, sliced
a small turnip, cubed
mixed herbs to taste
black pepper
1 kg small whole potatoes

Remove **all** fat from lamb. Over low heat, brown
the meat and onions in a non-stick saucepan with
a little of the stock. Add the carrots and turnip,
herbs and pepper. Cover with the remainder of the
stock and bring to the boil. Lower heat and
simmer for about 2 hours. Add the potatoes and
cook for a further 20 minutes. Serve with
wholemeal dumplings.

(Just to give credit where it's due, I've nicked this
dumpling recipe out of the National Heart
Foundation's cookbook, *Guide To Healthy Eating*
— I know a good dumpling recipe when I see
one.)

Dumplings

½ *cup wholemeal self raising flour*
½ *cup white self raising flour*
1 tablespoon polyunsaturated oil
1 egg, beaten
1 tablespoon skim milk

Combine flours and rub in oil. Mix in egg and milk to make a dry dough. Roll small pieces of dough between the palms of the hand to form a ball about 2.5 cm in diameter. Drop dumplings in stew about five minutes before it is finished.

BEEF

Meatball medley

(Serves 4)

500 g low-fat topside mince
½ onion, chopped
3 tablespoons low-fat evaporated milk
½ teaspoon nutmeg
½ cup rolled oats
seasoning
1 tablespoon polyunsaturated oil
2 brown onions, sliced
1 × 440 g can tomato purée, no added salt
4 medium potatoes, sliced
small packet frozen peas

Mix together mince, chopped onion, evaporated milk, nutmeg, oats and seasoning and form into small balls. Fry the sliced onion in a little of the oil and set aside. Brown the meatballs in the remaining oil and when done, add the purée and the sliced onions. Simmer over low heat for about 20 minutes. Add potato and cook a further 10 minutes. Add the peas and simmer until all the vegetables are cooked.

Stir fried beef

(Serves 4)

500 g round or boneless blade steak
2 teaspoons cornflour
2 teaspoons water
1 teaspoon sesame oil
1 tablespoon grapeseed or olive oil
2 small onions, quartered and separated
½ cup sliced celery
1 green capsicum and 1 red capsicum, sliced
½ cup sliced beans
1 clove garlic, crushed
1 teaspoon grated fresh ginger
1 cup sliced mushrooms
½ cup fresh bean sprouts
1 tablespoon low-salt soy sauce
2 tablespoons sherry
¼ cup beef stock

Trim steak and cut into long, thin strips. Place in a
bowl with cornflour, water and sesame oil. Mix
thoroughly, then set aside and leave for 30
minutes. Heat the grapeseed or olive oil in a wok
or large pan and add onion, celery, capsicums and
beans. Stir fry until vegetables are cooked but still
crisp. Remove from wok and keep warm. Place
garlic and ginger in wok. Stir, then add the
mushrooms and beef. Stir-fry on high until beef

changes colour. Return vegetables to wok, add the bean sprouts and stir. Blend soy, sherry and stock. Pour into pan and stir until heated through. Serve on noodles.

French pot roast

(Serves 6–8)

1–1½ kg beef (preferably topside or bolar)
1 tablespoon olive oil
2 onions, finely chopped
2 cloves garlic, crushed
6 medium carrots, finely chopped
3 sticks celery, finely sliced
12 mushrooms, finely chopped
1 teaspoon lemon juice
1½ cups beef stock or water
½ cup red wine
1½ tablespoons flour
2 bay leaves
½ teaspoon dried thyme
2 tablespoons tomato paste
350 g sliced potatoes
200 g peas
freshly ground black pepper to taste

Trim the meat of **all** fat and brown in the oil over high heat in a heavy bottomed saucepan. Remove and set aside. Lower the heat and fry onions and garlic in the same oil for about 3 minutes. Drain off surplus fat or oil. Add the carrots, celery, mushrooms and lemon juice and continue cooking for 5 minutes. Heat the stock and wine. Stir flour into vegetables in saucepan and add the warm stock and wine. Replace the beef in the pan, add herbs, tomato paste and pepper and simmer over a low heat until tender, about 2½ hours. Add the potatoes and peas and simmer for further 20–25 minutes.

Beef and potato curry

(Serves 4–6)

500–750g chuck steak
2 tablespoons seasoned flour
1–1½ tablespoons oil
2 medium onions, chopped
2 cloves garlic, crushed
3 cm piece of fresh green ginger, peeled and
 chopped
2 green chilies, chopped
¼ teaspoon hot chili powder
1 teaspoon garam masala
1 tablespoon tumeric
1 teaspoon ground cumin
½ teaspoon ground cloves
2 tablespoons crushed cardamom seeds
1 teaspoon ground coriander
2 tablespoons tomato paste, no added salt
rind and juice of ½ lemon
2 bay leaves
2 cups water
500 g potatoes, scrubbed and sliced

Trim and cube the meat and toss in seasoned flour.
Heat oil in a large saucepan and quickly brown the
meat. Remove meat from pan. Put onions and
garlic in pan and fry, stirring occasionally until the
onions are golden brown. Add the ginger and

chilies and cook for 4 minutes, stirring frequently. Stir in the spices and cook for further 6 minutes, stirring frequently. Add the tomato paste, stir and then add the meat, lemon juice and rind and bay leaves. Stir in the water and bring to the boil. Cover the meat and reduce the heat to low and simmer the mixture for 1¼ hours. Add the potatoes and bring to boil again. Re-cover and simmer for further 30 minutes, or until meat is cooked and potatoes are cooked through.

Pasta

Pasta is very easily cooked in the microwave and it doesn't become 'gooey'. It can be served with a number of sauces.

Meat sauce
(Serves 4)

250 g lean mince beef (topside)
1 onion, sliced
1 tablespoon polyunsaturated margarine
1 carrot
1 small piece celery
100 g mushrooms
1 teaspoon oregano
sprinkling fresh parsley, finely chopped
1 tablespoon flour
seasoning
pinch of cinnamon
1 tablespoon concentrated tomato paste
½ cup white wine
300 ml stock

Brown onion in the margarine. Add the other vegetables, the oregano and parsley. When these are browned, put in the meat. Stir well so that it is evenly browned. Sprinkle in the flour, seasoning and cinnamon, then add tomato paste, heated wine and about 300 mls stock. Simmer for 40 minutes, uncovered. Serve over spaghetti with a little grated Parmesan.

Neapolitan tomato sauce

(Serves 4)

1 tablespoon polyunsaturated oil
1 onion, chopped
2 cloves garlic, crushed
fresh basil or parsley to taste
2 slices ham (optional), chopped
4–6 tomatoes, peeled and seeded
freshly ground black pepper

Heat oil, add onion and garlic and cook until
clear. Add ham and rest of ingredients. Cook over
slow heat for about 8 minutes. Serve over pasta,
sprinkled with a little Parmesan cheese.

Can also be used over fish (exclude ham).

Tomato sauce with marsala

(Serves 2–3)

500 g tomatoes (peeled) or tinned tomatoes
1 onion, chopped
1 clove garlic, crushed
1 sherry glass of marsala

Cook all ingredients except marsala for 5 minutes, stirring occasionally. Add the marsala and cook a further 2 or 3 minutes, stirring. Serve over pasta, fish or meat.

Microwave spinach and pine nut sauce

(Serves 3–4)

250 g spinach
1 cup parsley, chopped
4 shallots, chopped
1 teaspoon polyunsaturated margarine
1 tablespoon flour
1 cup low-fat milk
seasoning
½ cup pine nuts

Wash spinach and place in a freezer bag. Place in microwave and cook on high for about 4 minutes. Drain and purée with the parsley and shallots. Put the margarine in a bowl and melt (microwave on high for about 45 seconds). Stir in the flour, seasoning and milk and cook for 2–3 minutes until thickened, stirring often. Add the spinach mixture and pine nuts and heat on medium for 2 minutes, stirring occasionally. Serve with pasta.

Mussel sauce

(Serves 4)

1½ kg fresh mussels
a little polyunsaturated oil
1 onion, chopped
2–3 cloves garlic, crushed
725 g tomatoes, peeled and chopped (or
mixture of tomato purée and tomatoes)
½ teaspoon each of dried marjoram and
thyme
handful chopped parsley
pepper

Scrub the shellfish and remove beards and all grit.
Put them into a covered pan over high heat and let
the shells open. Discard any that do not open.
Strain, and remove the mussels from the shells. Set
aside. In the warmed oil, sauté the chopped onion
and the garlic. Add the chopped tomatoes and
when slightly reduced add the mussels and a
handful of chopped parsley. As soon as the dish is
hot, pour over spaghetti and serve **without** cheese.

Largely Vegetarian

Microwave curried vegetables
(Serves 4)

1 tablespoon oil
1 medium onion, chopped
1 clove garlic, crushed
1 teaspoon mustard seeds
2 tablespoons curry powder
1 cm grated fresh ginger
3 cups mixed vegetables (any combination of
*   root vegetables and pumpkin), chopped*
1 cup beans, sliced
1 cup small cauliflower florets or broccoli

Heat oil in a medium-sized microwave dish for 1
minute. Add onion and garlic. Cook for about 2
minutes. Add the mustard seeds, curry and ginger
and cook a further minute. Add the mixed
vegetables and cover with plastic wrap or a lid and
cook for about 4 minutes, stirring several times.
Stir in remaining vegetables. Cover and cook for
6–7 minutes, stirring occasionally. Serve with rice.

Stuffed tomatoes

(Serves 4)

4 large tomatoes
2 slices wholemeal bread
1 clove garlic, cut
1 tablespoon grapeseed oil
2 generous tablespoons chopped parsley
pepper

Halve tomatoes and remove the pulp. Remove the crusts from the bread and rub on both sides with the clove of garlic and the oil and leave for a few minutes. Cube the bread, then mix with the parsley and season. Pack the bread into the tomatoes. Place in an ovenproof dish and cook slowly under the grill until browned. Serve as a luncheon dish with salad or as an accompaniment to grills.

Baked aubergines (egg plant) with tomatoes

(Serves 4)

200 g zucchini
240 g aubergines (eggplant)
360 g tomatoes
200 g mushrooms
½ teaspoon thyme
clove garlic, chopped
2 teaspoons polyunsaturated oil
pepper

Preheat oven to 200°C. Give the zucchini and eggplant a striped effect by peeling them along their length with a potato peeler, leaving strips of skin about 1 cm wide all the way down. Cut them into thin slices. Clean the mushrooms and cut into slices. Slice the tomatoes thinly. Arrange all the vegetables in ovenproof dish, overlapping them and alternating the colours. Sprinkle vegetables with the thyme, garlic, oil and seasoning. Cover with foil and cook for about 30 minutes.

Sweets

Fruit jelly with mint cream
(Serves 4–6)

Fruit jelly

2 × 440 g tins of berries
4 sprigs mint
1 tablespoon lemon juice
3 teaspoons (1 envelope) gelatine
2 tablespoons water
1 dessertspoon port

Strain the juice from the fruit, reserving the fruit.
Heat the juice and the sprigs of mint together and
simmer for a few minutes. Allow to cool. Add the
lemon juice. Meanwhile, line a jelly mould with
plastic wrap. Place the gelatine in a bowl. Add the

two tablespoons of water and place the bowl in a pan of simmering water until the gelatine completely dissolves. Remove the mint leaves from the syrup, pour the syrup onto the gelatine and then add the fruit and port. Fill the mould with this mixture. Leave to set in refrigerator for 3–4 hours.

Mint cream ingredients

approximately 10 mint leaves
1 tablespoon lemon juice
250 ml low-fat natural yoghurt (sweetened with a little sugar or artificial sweetener)
mint and berries for decoration

Crush the mint with the lemon juice. Add the yoghurt and stir. Serve with jelly decorated with berries and extra mint.

Apple and mango jelly

(Serves 4)

1 sachet of gelatine
350 ml clear apple juice
¼ cup clear liqueur (kirsch, cointreau)
1 tin mango (or fresh if available — sliced)
8 leaves and 4 sprigs mint

Sprinkle the gelatine over the apple juice and liqueur in a saucepan. Heat gently and stir the mixture until clear and the gelatine has dissolved. Pour a little of this mixture into four moulds and place in refrigerator. When they have set, arrange a mango segment in each mould and a mint leaf on the top. Pour in a little more jelly and allow to set. Add another segment of fruit and a mint leaf and then more jelly. The fruit should be covered by jelly. Chill until completely set. To serve, unmould and garnish with sprigs of mint.

Sherried peaches

(Serves 4)

½ cup mashed fresh peach flesh
2 tablespoons almonds, chopped
½ teaspoon almond essence
¼ cup sherry
4 fresh peaches
low-fat natural yoghurt (sweetened with a little honey or artificial sweetener)

Mix together mashed peach, almonds, essence and sherry. Cover and leave in the refrigerator for 24 hours. Peel and slice the peaches, place in bowl and pour the prepared mixture over the top. Serve with the yoghurt.

Fresh fruit compote

(Serves 6)

1 small pineapple, peeled and diced
3 peaches, peeled and sliced
½ cup blueberries
¼ cup blanched almonds
½ cup syrup made from imitation sweetener or
*   sugar and water*
¼ cup kirsch
1 teaspoon sugar

Mix the fruit and nuts together, pour syrup over
these and sprinkle with the kirsch. Chill well
before serving.

Melon and raspberry compote

(Serves 4–6)

500 g ripe raspberries
2 tablespoons kirsch
sugar to taste (optional)
1 ripe honeydew melon

Sprinkle the raspberries with the kirsch and sugar
(if wanted) and chill for several hours. Remove the
melon flesh, dice, and combine it with the
raspberries.

Microwave quick Christmas pudding

(Serves 4)

2 tablespoons polyunsaturated margarine
2½ tablespoons brown sugar
2 cups fruit medley
1 cup low-fat milk
1 tablespoon jam
1 teaspoon bicarbonate soda
1 cup self raising flour
2 teaspoons cocoa
nutmeg, spices, etc
2 tablespoons rum, brandy or sherry for
*   cooking and a little brandy for a final touch*

Mix the first five ingredients together in a
microwave jug or in a plastic pudding-shaped
bowl. Bring to the boil on high. Immediately add
the bicarbonate soda, then mix in the flour, cocoa
and spices. Add the liquor and microwave,
covered with plastic wrap (microwave proof), for
12 minutes on medium. Sprinkle with extra
brandy before serving.